Y0-BDD-246

Living Through Loving

Reflections on Letters of the New Testament

Leslie F. Brandt

Publishing House
St. Louis London

Concordia Publishing House, St. Louis, Missouri
Concordia Publishing House Ltd., London, E. C. 1

Library of Congress Catalog Card No. 73-88949
ISBN 0-570-03173-7

MANUFACTURED IN THE UNITED STATES OF AMERICA

Contents

Romans 5

The truth of the matter is—
    and this in spite of those fine, religious people
    who attempt to placate God
    by means of laws and rules
    and traditions and customs—
    the truth of the matter is
    that we *have been* accepted by God
    through Jesus Christ.
This is where we now stand.
And this is what we ought to celebrate.
We can well afford to celebrate this
    even amid the difficult circumstances that plague us.
Whether it be physical pain or mental anguish,
    material loss or excruciating sorrow,
    this does not separate us from God,
    nor alter our relationship to Him.
It is when we accept and cling to what God has done
    for us through Christ,
    irrespective of our human feelings and frailties,
    that the very conflicts that beset us,
    and may even threaten to destroy us,
    become God's tools
    to grind and polish and temper our spirits
    and prepare us for loving and obedient service.
This is no vain hope;
    it's the Gospel truth.
God's love and Spirit *do* abide within us.

This is not something we have earned or merited.
We were estranged from God, the enemies of God,
    from the very beginning.

And it was for God's enemies that Christ died.
It will always be a great mystery,
something we can never quite comprehend,
but it was this One, the Christ,
who reconciled us to God.
What we cannot comprehend, we can still celebrate.
For it was through this sacrifice of our Lord,
God's act of grace and gift of love,
that we have been made
the very sons and daughters of God.
We may not know exactly
how or when sin entered our world.
We do know that all men are sinners—
that disease and death, physical and spiritual,
have permeated the whole human race.
The laws of God,
and the precepts of men
who tried to find and follow God,
were initiated to bring order into humanity's chaos.
And it was these ancient laws that revealed to man
his inner sickness and eternal estrangement
from his Creator.

God's love for man, however, is far greater
than the evil that brings death and destruction.
God's grace is more powerful than man's wickedness.
It was this that was revealed through Jesus Christ,
and it is this that grants us eternal life.

Romans 6

Regardless of our past,
no matter how atrocious our wrongdoings,
whether our sins be unconscious or even deliberate,
our Lord's sacrifice is sufficient
and God's forgiveness complete.
Whereas we shall always be sinners,
and failures will plague us from time to time,
the forgiven and reconciled children of God
will dedicate themselves to obedience and good works.

We are now, even as sinners,
the sons and daughters of righteousness.
We have, in effect, been crucified with Christ
and raised with Him from the dead.
We are new people,
focused upon new goals,
compelled by new ambitions,
committed to new objectives.

This means that we cease yielding to self-interest
and self-concern,
seeking our own gratification at the expense of others.
This is the way we lived in the past.
We have now been reborn.
All things have become new.
Having received the gift of God's love,
we love and accept ourselves
because God loves and accepts us,
and we dedicate ourselves
to loving our fellowmen as ourselves.

Whereas we were once slaves to self-concern,
we are now set free from its destructive bondage
to be the followers of Jesus Christ.
While we celebrate our redemption,
even while we fail at times
to reflect and communicate the loving grace of God,
this is the stand we take,
and this is the goal we pursue.

We have discovered through sad experience
that there is nothing to be gained
through self-service.
It resolves only in disillusionment and aching emptiness.
The gift of God is life forever.
Service to God,
and to our fellowman for God's sake and by His grace,
fills life with joy and meaning and purpose.

Romans 7

Our primary allegiance is no longer to a rigid set
of dos and don'ts.
This is the way some people live;
they mouth and claim to adhere
to the Ten Commandments
or some vague system of morality
of their own making.
This is what they worship;
in such they find their security.
It is this, they feel,
that makes them acceptable to God.

Rules and laws are necessary
to any community or society.
They teach unregenerate men
how to live and work together.
They curb our selfishness and protect our investments.
And they keep us from destroying each other.
They may even serve to reveal our human frailties
and make us aware of our self-centered aspirations.
They point up man's estrangement from his Creator,
how out of orbit and powerless his life really is.
But they can in no way restore a man to God.

Our allegiance is to God through Jesus Christ.
Our relationship to Him is based not on what
we have done for God,
but on what He has done on our behalf.
Christ has measured up to God's standards
and has taken upon Himself
the penalty for our imperfections.

We have been declared righteous, perfect in Christ,
apart from the laws
that are needed to govern our lives.
We still need laws to direct and protect
the lives and destinies of men,
but they are incapable
of turning sinners into saints.

The ancient laws do, indeed, portray
goodness and justice.
They portray as well
my utter inability to be truly good and just.
I simply do not have within my nature the capability
of reaching those great standards.
God knows that I have tried.
He knows, as well, how again and again I miserably fail.
I have the desire, even the will, to do what is right.
I do not, in myself, have the power.
And thus there is conflict, agonizing conflict,
and I am driven to the wall in despair.
It is a conflict which, in one measure or another,
will persist as long as I live upon this world.

The answer is in Jesus Christ.
God, through this Christ, adopted me as His son
apart from the Law.
I am set free from the Law's demands,
and free from its judgment,
free to immerse myself in God's great love,
and free to serve Him forever.

Romans 8

It's the truth; it's a fact!
We need only to claim it and celebrate it!
We are not to be judged under the Law,
nor are we to be condemned in our Law-breaking.
When we accept what God has done for us through Christ
we are delivered completely and forever
from the guilt of sin.
It is just as if sin never happened.
This is what Christ did for us
some two thousand years ago.
In the moment that we lay claim to God's great gift
of forgiving love,
it is applicable to us—here and now.
What laws and morals and rules and regulations
can never do,
God has done on our behalf.

And it is this that makes us
the very sons and daughters of God.
It is this, perpetuated by His Spirit within us,
that enables us to turn from self-service
and its resultant estrangement from God
to godly service and love of our fellowman
and to fulfillment and everlasting happiness as well.
It is this that makes life significant, meaningful,
and gives point and purpose to our living.

It is this
that puts us back into God's orbit for our lives
and welds us to Him
in a union that no one can dissolve.

Nothing, nothing at all,
can come between us and our loving God.
Our feelings of guilt and depression
will rise and haunt us,
but they will in no way alter
God's redeeming and accepting love.
Not, that is,
unless we live in accord with such foolish feelings
and neglect to hear and abide by God's Word.
The tragedies and conflicts of this life
will discourage us,
but they can in no way change God's attitudes
or stifle His love for us.
Failures and defeats may trip us up,
but such do not affect our relationship to God.
Our boat will rock, the earth will tremble.
Revolutions will shake up governments and institutions.
Our traditions may be nullified,
our convictions threatened.
Every temporal security may crumble.
But God's love and reconciling grace are forever,
and He will never let us go.
If our allegiance is to God and our faith fixed on Him,
the very atrocities that seek to destroy us
become the means
by which He carries out His will
in us and through us.

Nothing, absolutely nothing
can separate us from the love of God
as revealed and proclaimed and demonstrated
through Jesus Christ.
We are the sons and daughters of God,
His servants and disciples forever.

Romans 12

Celebration must be combined with service.
The relationship between man and God is a two-way street.
Our great God gives;
    we must respond to His gracious gifts.
Our response is the offering of our lives,
    the placing of ourselves at His disposal,
    for the accomplishment of His purposes
    in our world about us.
We are, once we acknowledge God's love
    and accept His salvation,
    under new management.
This is what worship is all about.
It is not confined
    to loud singing or verbal exclamations.
It is turning our hearts, minds, and bodies
    over to God's ownership,
    and dedicating our abilities and gifts to His service.

We have all received such gifts for this very purpose.
They are not given to us to enhance our beauty
    or assure our worldly security,
    or even to make us more desirable or respected
    among the people with whom we live and labor.
They are committed to us
    in order to be committed back to God
    in and through and by way of service
    to our fellowmen for God's sake.
This is precisely the way in which our God meets
    the needs of our neighbor—through us
    and through these gifts entrusted to us.

Not all of us have those gifts that enable us
to administer or preach
or teach or finance important projects.
But we all have specific abilities—
love, energy, persistence, patience,
sincerity, concern, creativity.
We are to exercise these things upon one another
and on behalf of one another.
We are to care for each other
even as much as we care for ourselves.
We are to allow our God to reach and touch others,
even our very enemies,
with His care and concern for them through us.

Romans 13

We are God's children now.
We have been set free
    from the stern requirements of the Law,
    even the screaming demands
    of our self-centered natures,
    in order to live and celebrate and serve
    as God's sons and daughters.
But we are to live responsibly.
Even the secular authorities over us
    are to be God's instruments
    through which He governs and directs our lives.
When we disobey such,
    or fail to perform our obligations to such,
    we must suffer the penalty for our disobedience.

Nevertheless, our responsibility
    is first and foremost to God.
The authorities we choose to govern us
    must be expected to govern in accordance
    with His goals and objectives.
If their rule is unjust,
    we must seek to bring justice to all men.
If they seek to usurp God's will for our lives,
    we must obey God in scorn of consequences.
They may be God's instruments,
    but they can by no means
    take God's place in our lives
    and force us to carry out
    their wishes and objectives
    that run contrary to God's will and Word for us.

We must surely respect our governing authorities,
but God forbid that we deify them
or assume that they always speak for God
in respect to our lives
or the welfare of humanity about us.

We have been set free from the demands of the Law
In order to relate to and be governed by a higher,
more perfect law.
It is the law or the requirement of love.
We are to love God, and we are to love our fellowman—
every fellowman—even as we love ourselves.
We are to love, and are enabled to love,
because God first loved us
and demonstrated that love through Jesus Christ.
Let us demonstrate love in our fractured world,
and love as God would have us love.
Let us live for God and for others
rather than for ourselves.

Romans 14

No matter how strong our convictions,
    or how ecstatic our feelings in respect to our faith,
    God forbid that we attempt to compress Him
    into set forms or shapes that we expect others
    to swallow and digest.
God is too big for our little boxes
    or our personal concoctions.
Whereas He is most certainly revealed through Christ,
    He is not confined to the regulations and revelations
    that we wrap around Him.
What may be good for us
    in respect to the means and methods
    of sustaining and demonstrating our faith
    is not necessarily appropriate for others.

We simply are not capable of passing judgment
    on the experience of another man.
His salvation must come through Jesus Christ.
The manner by which it comes,
    or the manner in which a person expresses his faith,
    is between him and his God.
Nor would we allow our relationship to God
    to be determined or threatened
    by another man's prerequisites.
Our love for one another ought to be generous enough
    to embrace the other
    regardless of the manner
    in which we assume to comprehend
    or endeavor to worship our God.
On the other hand,
    while we must cease to pass judgment upon the

actions of our fellowmen,
we have no license to flaunt our freedom
in ways that may threaten their faith
or cause them to flounder.

While others cannot dictate
what I can or cannot do as a Christian,
Christian love will not permit me
to unnecessarily
hurt or offend them.
My freedom in Christ gives me the freedom
to respect another man's convictions
even if they don't make sense to me.
Few of us will agree on all interpretations of God
and His will for our lives.
We can and must agree on the prime requirement
of every Christian,
that we learn how to love and care for one another.

Romans 15

Without compromising our own basic convictions
let us work for peace and unity
in our daily relationships.
How ridiculous, how infantile it is
to allow these convictions
to build up walls between us!
Why is it so difficult to accept another as he is—
without insisting that he come our way
or meet our standards?
After all, none of us fully comprehends God,
even as He is revealed through Jesus Christ.
So much of our faith is intermixed
with how we *feel* about God
and His will for our lives,
and is affected by our personal idiosyncrasies,
by the circumstances and influences that blend
to make us what we are.
This differs with each one of us.

Our first concern ought not to be for ourselves,
but for our neighbor, his needs and concerns.
We are not to play God in his life,
determining his goals and dictating his actions,
but the role of comrade, friend and brother,
seeking together, ever learning from each other,
what is God's best for us individually and mutually.
As we do this,
we will discover that our areas of agreement
are far more significant than are those things
in which we cannot agree,

and we will lovingly unite in celebrating God's love
and in carrying out His purposes.

To state it most simply,
we need to accept one another in the manner
that Christ has accepted each of us.
If we did this,
we would indeed find so much to celebrate.
Our lives would light up with praise rather than darken
our disjointed world with further disunity,
and lost men about us might see something
of the love and joy
that their hearts are grappling for.

1 Corinthians 1

It is amazing to me how in our immaturity
we tend to interpret God and to structure our faith
according to the precepts and pronouncements
of our human leaders.
There is no doubt that God does speak through such.
How else can He relate His wisdom and will
to His creatures
except by the accumulated experiences and insights
of His many servants throughout the centuries?
Nevertheless, there is a fearful risk in placing
all our eggs into one basket,
in tying our nerve endings to one or two powerful
or charismatic personalities that impress us
as God's very special saints and servants.
If our understanding of the Christian faith has
been pursued in this manner,
it is probably very limited, even distorted,
and we may end up with some human concoction
about God and His will for our lives.

However men may interpret it,
God reveals His love and redeeming power
through Christ and His cross.
When self-appointed interpreters attempt to go beyond
proclamation into some rational or human explanation,
to subdue or dilute its offensiveness,
to dissect its mystery,
or even to add to it
something that was never intended,
they come out as confusers rather than articulators
and confound rather than clarify the purposes of God.

The fact is clear: Christ died for our sins.
We are reconciled to our loving God through this Christ.
Nonsensical to some, offensive to others,
it remains for us proof positive of our relationship
to a living God,
our perpetual and eternal acceptance as His
sons and daughters.

Whereas God may use, even speak through,
the very gifted personalities about us,
the powerful, the affluential,
the very bright and talented people that pull down
the spotlights upon themselves
and occupy the great pulpits and stages of our world,
history bears witness
that God has more often revealed His purposes
through men and women who were rejected,
despised, imprisoned—even martyred—
by the community in which they lived.

Whatever the world may think about us,
God chose us, however weak or foolish
or failure fraught.
He has, through Christ, set us free from sin,
even our subjective feelings about ourselves,
to be His people—and to serve Him forever.

1 Corinthians 3 and 4

It is high time that we who are God's servants
leave our milk diet of subjective ecstasy
for the meat of basic discipleship.
We no longer have to play the numbers game.
Our great God does not judge our worth
by human standards.
Nor should we.
We do not have to always *feel* good
about our accomplishments.
Nor should we need the ego lift of popular acclaim
or the plaudits of our peers.
We, each one of us, have a job to do,
and we assume our responsibilities in accordance
with the guidance, the gifts, and the opportunities
that our God makes available to us.
As long as we are faithful to our task
and in our witness,
whether we lay foundations for others to build upon
or build upon those that have already been laid,
we are the workmen of God,
and God alone knows the true value and effectiveness
of our efforts.

The point is, our validity is not dependent
upon visible successes.
It is granted and stated by God Himself.
After all,
we are the vessels and vehicles of His Spirit,
His visible hands and feet
destined to perform His purposes.

The wisdom, the power, the ability
  to carry out His objectives
  all come from Him.
We are to take our orders from Him
  and give credit to whom credit is due.

Indeed, it is quite possible that our efforts
  to accomplish God's purposes
  will be condemned most severely by our fellowmen.
There are times when we may have to say and to do
  what we deeply feel He would have us say and do,
  and let the chips fall where they may.
And it is possible
  that, due to our human foibles and fallibilities,
  we may interpret incorrectly God's will
  and err in our endeavors to advance His kingdom.
Nevertheless, it is better
  to be subjected to the judgment
  of a loving, forgiving God
  than to submit to the condemnation
  of our equally fallible brothers and sisters.

How important it is to relate continually
  to the value judgments of our God!
If we seriously embrace the commission of Christ,
  we cannot begin to imagine to what heights or depths
  our discipleship will take us.
There will be moments on the mount.
There will be hours down in the valley—
  down where there is no honor or recognition,
  only loneliness and persecution,
  even suffering and imprisonment,
  as we seek to identify with the victims

of war and poverty and oppression and injustice,
and to communicate the love and healing of Christ
to those who need it the most.

Whatever the rewards for faithful service
in some future dispensation,
we are the sons and daughters,
disciples and servants of God.

Our appointment as such is reward enough.

God grant
that we may be loving and faithful and obedient.

1 Corinthians 12

Pentecost was a great deal more than wind and fire,
or even the utterance of strange languages
by uneducated tongues.
The ascension or disappearance of Jesus did not signify
God's departure from this world.
It was to prepare the way for His entrance into
and His indwelling within
the hearts of every one of His children.
God, incarnate in Jesus Christ,
is now incarnate within a new body,
the body of His church,
His sons and daughters commissioned
to advance His kingdom through all the earth.
And with the gift of His Spirit
are those great spiritual gifts
that enable us to carry out God's purposes.

The gifts of the Spirit differ,
and so do the people who possess them.
The Spirit, however, is One and the same,
and this makes every one of God's children
of equal value and importance to God.
The more popular gifts are not the most significant,
even if they are sought out
and applauded by the multitudes.
Whether they are recognized as gifts
of preaching or healing
or writing or administrating,
or in more profound terms
of loving patience, enduring scholarship
or courageous daring,

whether they be the gifts of intelligence or insight,
making money or making music,
they all come from God, these gifts, and His Spirit
remains the same Spirit in the heart of every man.

It is unfortunate that, according to worldly standards,
the one who articulates well or sings impressively
or performs skillfully on a musical instrument
or rates high in some sport
or captures the imagination and loyalty of the masses
through capable leadership
attracts the most attention and makes the headlines.
Other gifts, equally important but less visible,
are often little recognized or appreciated.
This ought not to be so
in respect to the gifts of the Spirit.
Nor do the more popular gifts indicate a greater measure
of spiritual power or of the Spirit's presence.
The church constitutes the body of Christ,
and the body, in order to function well,
demands the faithful and obedient response
of all its members.
God forbid that it be all mouth to speak or feet to run.
All parts must be honored and respected and allowed
to perform their various functions.
And God forbid that we set our hearts
on gifts of our own choosing.

There are more important gifts to reach for,
and they are available to every one who will
allow the Spirit total access to his body and being.
Above all is the grace to love one another,
to share with one another, and to help one another
in the way of our Lord and Savior, Jesus Christ.

1 Corinthians 13

The ability to be truly loving people
is the greatest gift of all.
It is that gift which most of us appear to possess
in such small measure.
We talk a good deal about it;
we make grand statements concerning it.
But when the chips are down, we usually find our vaunted
love in short supply.

We have little difficulty in loving those who love us,
or in showing some concern for those who will
respond favorably to our investments in them.
If the time and place are right,
we are even capable
of risking our lives and possessions
in behalf of a brother who is in trouble.
Whatever the reason—
chivalry, honor, pride, or simple reflex action—
our world harbors many heroes.
True lovers, however, are few and far between.

The true lovers are the people who are empowered
and motivated by the love of God.
Theirs is a selfless, truth-seeking, all-enduring love.
They love in the measure that they acknowledge
and experience God's love for them.
They discover that their response to divine love
must be demonstrated
in their relationship to humanity about them.
Most of the fantastic gifts that appeal to the masses
are temporal and terminal.

Love, authentic love, is eternal,
    and propagates and perpetuates love.
The ability to love is truly the supreme gift—
    the gift to which we all should aspire.

I remember well the honeymoon stage
    of my Christian experience,
    those beautiful years when love was mostly vertical,
    and I sincerely felt I was "in love" with God.
I am glad for those years,
    and for the thrill and ecstasy of countless hours
    spent alone with God.
And yet I had little understanding of what it meant
    to love, as Jesus loved,
    the poor and the oppressed,
    the refugees, the disenfranchised.
I was anxious that people might turn from darkness
    to light, from sin to salvation.
But I was insensitive to the physical and mental hurts
    that plagued a billion creatures in the same world
    in which I lived.

Now that I am growing up,
    I am slowly learning how to love
    and that loving God is demonstrated
    in loving my brothers and sisters about me,
    that God has chosen to relate His love to this world
    through me and others who have laid claim
    and committed themselves to His love.
My ability to love is still short-circuited
    by self-centeredness.
I know it is only as I rest in His love for me
    that I will learn how to respond in love to others.

1 Corinthians 14

More than anything else in heaven or on earth,
I pray for the power to love my fellowman,
to break through the damning bigotry,
the crippling prejudice,
the stifling self-centeredness
that smothers God's Spirit within me,
and to channel and communicate divine love
to lonely, loveless people about me.
And I pray as well for the ability to translate
the message of God's eternal love into words
that will pierce the benumbed minds of busy men
and move their hearts to faith and obedience.

While others may revel in the language of ecstasy,
I covet the gift of speaking and writing
lucidly in the language of my fellowmen.
Whereas a sign or symbol
of the Spirit's presence and power
may well take the form of strange, ecstatic sounds
and may even stimulate God's servants
to more radical obedience,
it is far better that we aspire to those gifts
that will more emphatically proclaim God's love
and reveal His concern for the human family.
The special, ecstatic experiences,
and the sounds that reveal those experiences,
may serve well to bathe dull lives in exquisite joy
and be of some value in one's private meditations,
but the gifts that enable God's servants
to advance His kingdom on earth
are the gifts of sacrificial love,

steadfast faith
and courageous obedience that compels Christians
to live, even to die,
for the sake of Christ
and the salvation of their fellowmen.
What all of us who follow Christ
ought to covet most of all is that quality of love
that goes beyond verbal witness and proclamation
to the dedication of our energies and talents,
even our very lives,
to the bodily welfare and spiritual salvation
of humanity throughout the world.
If our love or concern for others falls short of this,
it falls short of our Lord's requirements
for an obedient and effective disciple.

It is necessary that we grow up in our thinking
about spiritual matters,
and in our understanding about spiritual values.
The church needs the more mature gifts
if it is to reach men and women
with the message of God's love in Christ.
Those abilities, whatever their source,
that do not benefit the church
or enhance the body of Christ
are of little value to the enterprise of God.
We need not deny the gifts or experiences of others—
even if we do not understand them
and may not even desire them for ourselves.
We must, however, concentrate upon those things
that will give meaning and significance
for our ministry to our fellowmen.

2 Corinthians 3

The saints of the Old Testament assumed that the scent
that ascended heavenward from the animal offerings
that fried on their altar fires
was sweet in the nostrils of God.
It may have been.
Sacrifices of another sort, however,
are required from God's saints of this day.
It is the aroma of these sacrifices which permeates
the world of this hour.
It brings joy and light and salvation to some people.
Others it offends and turns them into outright rebels
who disavow God and perish in darkness.
We are called to be such saints and sacrifices.
The power to thus affect our world
and to transform the lives of people about us
does not come out of ourselves.
It is God's power and comes to us
and to others through us
by way of His ever-present Spirit within us.

This power, this divine scent,
is released only by sacrifice,
the offering of our very lives
on the altar of humanity's need.
We are not assigned to demonstrate
a new law or discipline.
Nor are we expected to pass out formulas
for proper living.
We are here to proclaim and to demonstrate Jesus Christ,
the forgiving love and eternal freedom that was
released to all men through His great sacrifice.

This is the reason that we, the servants of God,
the disciples of Christ,
are the hope of our world today.
We can slice through the blindness
of men's unbelieving hearts
and reveal the glory of God's great gift of life
and set them free for celebration and service.
We cannot do this, however, by peddling the good news
as newsboys peddle papers.
We are called upon to burn for our God,
to offer our lives,
to give of ourselves to our fellowman's needs,
and to let God take care of the consequences.

Not all men we serve in this manner
will respond in loving gratitude.
They may well crucify us as they crucified our Lord.
We have been set free from human ego-needs
for that glory which comes through Christ,
the freedom to live, or even to die,
that God's purposes may be accomplished through us
and His kingdom may grow around us.

2 Corinthians 4

We have been brainwashed into believing that
success is measured by statistics.
It is no wonder that depression sets in
when our successes cannot be counted on our fingers
or even tabulated on computers.
The kind of service to which we are assigned,
as well as the results of our faithful endeavors,
are fully known and understood by God.
Even our errors are known, understood,
accepted, and forgiven by God.
Discouragement will be our lot at times,
but we don't have to remain immobilized
by its tentacles.

We are vessels, clay pots, in the hands of God.
And every pot has its flaws.
God has chosen to deliver His eternal gifts
to this world through such vessels.
He may have to break and remake us from time to time,
but use us He will—with our permission.
He only requires that we gratefully submit
our beings and bodies for His use,
and consecrate our efforts and energies
for His purposes.

Of course we will have problems.
There will be times when we are flattened by despair.
There will probably be executioners about
trying to nail us to some cross.
Our premature death is a distinct possibility,
at least disgrace or imprisonment.

It is quite possible
    that we will lose our social status,
    home, job—perhaps even friends and family—
    if we dare to let God have His way with us.
Whatever we lose we will regain a thousandfold
    in this life or in the next.
This is the promise of our God.
And He hasn't short-changed anyone yet.

The truth is, we don't have to be discouraged.
We can be free even from fear of failure.
Only then are we free to live—or to die—
    to joyously spend and expend our lives
    for Jesus' sake.

2 Corinthians 5

The real basis for courage
    and the willingness to risk our lives
    as God's servants in this dispensation
    is our relationship to another
    and eternal dispensation.
In reality we have nothing to lose,
    for we have already gained everything as God's
    children and servants.
He has given us everlasting life.
Is it too much for Him to expect that we allow Him
    the use of our temporal minds and bodies
    in the few days or years we have before us?

They are precious,
    these few years we have upon this world.
They are all we can consciously comprehend.
But the same God
    who gave us this three-dimensional experience
    has promised us eternal dimensions
    beyond anything we can imagine or comprehend.
He asks only that we trust Him
    and demonstrate that trust in all-out commitment
    of all we are and have to Him
    and to our fellowman for His sake.
This is what faith is all about.
As a matter of fact,
    if we really knew what lay ahead of us
    in that eternal world that is to come,
    we would be too anxious to enter its portals
    and much too impatient about the few years

and many tasks and hard problems
of this temporal existence that crowd about us.

Anyway, we can stop being cowards
and begin taking risks for God.
We are the inheritors of His great kingdom,
heirs and joint heirs with Jesus Christ Himself.
Whatever we tenaciously hold on to in this life
eventually turns to ashes.
Whatever we painfully, responsibly,
and lovingly give away
really enhances our lives here;
and in the process of serving others
we serve our gracious God.
It is the risk we can well afford to take.

Galatians 4

We who are Christians need no longer be concerned
about identity crisis.
We are identified—and we have identity.
We are the sons and daughters of God.
To emphatically and eternally establish this fact,
God, through His Spirit,
entered our hearts and lives.
He redeemed us, adopted us, infilled and indwelt us.
We belong to Him; He is our Creator-Redeemer-Father.
This gives us infinite significance and worth.
And this gives us access to all the wealth and power
of His eternal kingdom.

This was not always true about the human family,
nor is it true even now about those who have
not embraced the life and salvation of Jesus Christ.
Man, created by God for the purposes of God,
chose the enslavement of the human will
and its desires.
He is not able, by himself,
to extricate himself from that enslavement.
Jesus Christ broke through the bars
of man's imprisonment
to bring him into the sunlight
of God's love and grace.
He freed him from self-will and reconciled him
to His heavenly Father once more.
Now we belong to the great family of God.

And yet it is still possible to lose that identity,
to foolishly and tragically give way to the unruly,

self-centered desires of the flesh
or the plaudits and commendations
of this temporal world.
If one chooses to live by sight rather than by faith,
to value the security of this life
or entrust himself to its demands
and covet its rewards
rather than submit to the loving will of God,
he leaves his Father's home and family
to become a wanderer lost
in the wilderness of this existence.
So let us choose Christ, not once
but every day of our lives.
This is really living!

Ephesians 1

Truly, we have much to celebrate
as the sons and daughters of God.
We have, through Christ, become the recipients
of God's whole treasurehouse of spiritual gifts.
Even before we were born—
before the world itself was made—
we were destined to be His children.

Christ's death on the cross
set us free from the Law's demands.
All charges against us were blotted out.
Our sins were forgiven.
Reconciled to the divine family,
we are now an integral part of God's plan
to reconcile the whole world to Him.
It is, indeed, something we cannot comprehend,
but God created us and chose us to be His people,
and this was God's purpose and plan
from the very beginning.
It was made known to us and made possible for us
through Jesus Christ.
Through Christ and His indwelling Spirit,
the brand of God's ownership was burned indelibly
into our hearts.
With the gracious gift of His Spirit is the guarantee
that all of God's gifts,
though at present unseen and little understood,
are already ours and will be revealed to us
in God's own time.

The power that is available to us,
  that resides within us,
  is beyond our wildest imaginations.
Subjected, as we are,
  to all the weaknesses and liabilities
  of our humanity,
  it is almost impossible to believe
  that this God-given power
  is the same power that raised Jesus from the dead.
And so we grovel in our frailties and failures
  rather than stand tall in our faith,
  assuming that our small problems
  are too great for God.

May the Spirit of God break through the numbness
  of our small thinking
  and reveal to us something
  of who we are and what we have become
  through Christ.
He is Lord over all, and we are His church, His body,
  the extension of this Christ in this world
  to which we are assigned.
How immeasurably and infinitely blessed we are!

Ephesians 2

It is truly amazing, almost breathtaking,
and ought to send us into paroxysms of ecstasy
when we take time to meditate
on what God has done for us.
We were once the children of darkness,
destined for destruction, the victims
of our own self-centered passions and desires,
but God, through Christ, reached into our murky cells
to bring us into the light, to make us alive.
Indeed, He has done it for every one of His creatures.
This is the glory and greatness of His grace.

While every human being is the object and beneficiary
of this divine gift of eternal love,
only those who by faith lay hold
of this divine offering,
who accept and live by this saving grace,
can discover and experience the salvation
that God has prepared for all men.
Whereas God's love is a gift which cannot be merited
by human efforts to aspire to divine standards,
God's deliverance from sin and self-service
sets us free to give our lives to good works,
to love God and to communicate love
to humanity about us.
This is, in one sense,
the real purpose for our salvation,
that we might serve God and fellowman
and thus fulfill that destiny
for which we were created.

It is God's love as manifested in Christ
    that makes us equal, in God's eyes, with all men.
And it makes all men equal with us.
We differ in many ways—
    in intellect, talents, training and temperament,
    background and opportunity.
Under God, however, there is no distinction.
His all-encompassing love levels all barriers
    and accounts every human creature
    of equal value and worth.
There are no strangers or aliens in God's family,
    only brothers and sisters.
And all of us are members of the one body,
    the body of Christ,
    and are commissioned to work together
    in carrying out His purposes.

Ephesians 4

If Christ is our Lord and Leader,
we had better set our sights on His prerequisites
and standards for our lives and strive to measure up.
For one thing,
it means that we be kind and gentle
and loving to one another.
After all, we are all members of the same body
and are motivated and guided by the same Spirit.
This is, at least, the way it ought to be—
unless some foreign spirit still possesses us
and hinders God's Spirit
from working out His purposes within us.
Why, then, is there so much bickering
among the children of God?
Like jealous, covetous siblings
we fight among ourselves,
jostling, crowding each other,
seeking position or honor above the other.
Our gifts, whatever they be, come from the hand of God.
They are not designed to give honor to one over another,
but, together with all who make up Christ's body,
to carry out His objectives and advance His kingdom
throughout the world.
They are granted to us, not to make us more important—
we already know our identity in Christ—
but for the purpose
of serving the human family about us.

It is time we stop acting like spoiled children,
pouting, griping, criticizing,
stepping on one another,

insisting on our way or scrambling for some power
or position that will boost our ego.
We ought to grow up, to be grateful for our status
as God's ministers,
whatever our parish or arena of service,
and relate to one another in truth and love.
Only then, as the body of Christ,
will we be truly effective
in our community and world.

Do you realize how difficult it sometimes is
to distinguish today's Christians
from the secularists of our world—
from the fun-seekers,
money-grabbers,
character-destroyers,
warmongers that make up the crowd around us?
Is it any wonder that the world is so short of lovers,
authentic lovers, redeemed and motivated by God,
who will apply the healing love of God
to the distortions of this world?
We may never be able to drown out all of our passions,
or rid ourselves of all our faults and weaknesses,
but we must cease doing those things
that hurt one another,
that limit our effectiveness as Christian ministers,
and learn how to be loving human beings.

Ephesians 5

Now we know that we are the children of God.
It follows, then, that we are responsible to Him,
to emulate Him, follow Him,
to soar within His orbit for our lives.
While we participate in what He has done for us,
it is expected that we imitate Him as well.
As God, through Christ, demonstrated His love for us,
so our lives, controlled by His love,
are to demonstrate such love toward our fellowman.

It is this that ought to determine our daily conduct.
The way we act or speak, the company we keep,
whatever we do—whether working or playing,
resting or recreating, eating or sleeping—
needs to be measured,
not by what most pleases us,
but in terms of what is pleasing to God
and what is most beneficial to our fellowmen.

The fact is, we are under new management, new orders.
Our primary task is now
to reflect, administer, communicate
God's infinite love
to a distorted and disjointed world.
While self-surrender underlines our relationship to God,
self-disclosure should characterize our relationship
toward our fellowmen.
While we are responsible to God alone,
and are not to be enslaved
by the demands of man or state,
we are, by divine commission,

enjoined to live honestly, openly, and lovingly
within our human family.

As the servants of God,
we need not and must not dedicate ourselves
to self-gratification.
The Spirit of God indwells our hearts.
With God's infilling and indwelling there is joy
beyond anything and everything this world can offer.
We are to claim that joy—and live within it—
rejoicing and celebrating with one another,
giving thanks to God for anything
that may come our way,
knowing that all things,
even the painful and tragic happenings of our lives,
will ultimately carry out God's purposes
in and through us.

With God's help, and because of His great love for us,
let us learn how to invest in one another—
to lovingly and sacrificially give of ourselves
to each other.
This is the key to genuine and everlasting joy
whatever the circumstances that crowd in upon us.

Philippians 1

I have met some beautiful people
in the course of my travels.
They are my sisters and brothers in Christ,
fellow servants in the kingdom-work of God.
Every time I think about them, I do so prayerfully,
and a surge of joy fills my heart.
God spoke to me, comforted me in my despair,
and through these people challenged me in my apathy.
I pray that God will continue to use them
to reach others
even as He used them to undergird and uplift me
and that what He has begun in us He will continue
until we are brought together
in everlasting fellowship
in that dimension beyond this life and world.

It is truly amazing to me,
and it should be encouraging to all of us,
the way in which God is able
to turn the unhappy things
that happen to us,
even our foolish errors and failures,
into stepping-stones toward the accomplishment
of His purposes in our world.
Even the apparent ego trips
of certain Christian evangelists,
who preach more for crowds than they do for Christ,
are sometimes utilized to promote the Gospel and
advance the cause of the Kingdom.
We have so much to celebrate.
God has not given up on our world.

He is here and sometimes because of us,
sometimes in spite of us,
He is working out His purposes in our world.

Our greatest concern at this point is
that we do not fail
to give God our all, and to risk our all,
that His purposes might be accomplished through us.
It means that we be willing
to put our lives on the line,
to live and, if need be, to die,
to fulfill our commission
as God's soldiers and servants.
We have nothing to lose and we have nothing
to be afraid of.
It is not surprising that we cling
so tenaciously to this life.
It is all that our natural senses can comprehend.
Nevertheless, if we knew what God has in store for us,
we would have no fear whatsoever of death
and whatever may follow death.
We would probably be most eager
to leave this vale of tears
for the indescribable glories of life eternal.
We are here in the valley under divine orders.
Let us be alive and courageous and joyful and obedient
as we faithfully carry out God's commission to us.

Philippians 2

There is a way to test the authenticity
of our relationship with God;
it is by examining our relationships
to our fellowmen.
If we are short on compassion and concern
for our brothers,
it must be that we haven't grasped or experienced
God's infinite love for us.
God is not holding back; His love is available.
And so is His great wealth and power and all
the other gifts needed to enrich our lives
and make us happy and secure.
They are, however, gifts
that must be shared with others
lest they turn to ashes in our hands.

There are, unfortunately, ambitious Christians
who are more concerned
about their own image
than the needs of their fellowman.
They attempt to corral their God-given gifts
for their own egocentric purposes.
This was not so with Jesus Christ.
Even though He was filled with the power of God,
He never used it for His own glory or gratification.
He became a servant of men,
using His divine power only to heal their hurts
and free their spirits and reveal to them
their rich inheritance as the children of God.
As God incarnate, Christ walked as man upon this earth—
even through the experiences of torture and death—

that He might touch human creatures
with the love of their Father in heaven.
Now we are assigned to be Christs incarnate—
proclaiming, demonstrating, and communicating
God's healing, reconciling love to one another
and to His wandering,
lonely, lost children around us.

We have wept and whined long enough.
It is time we claim God's proffered gifts
and begin to act responsively
as His divinely endowed servants.
Whereas we, as fallible human beings,
may claim the right to be imperfect,
we have, as well, the responsibility to focus
upon God's goals for our lives
and to become more and more
like the Christ who brought us to our God.
Now, as God's redeemed and restored children,
we are commissioned and assigned to brighten up
this dark world like stars that light up the night.
And like those stars that reflect the sun's glory
after darkness has fallen,
we are to spell out the promise of the coming dawn.
Our objective is the redemption of all men,
that every creature of God might honor the God
of his creation and be restored to His orbit
and destiny for his life.

Philippians 3

I suppose we must always be on our guard
against those sectarians and cultists
who wrap their lives
about their own private experiences and rituals
and then damn us
for not buying into their product.
We ought to be mature enough to avoid such entrapments.
We need to love these people,
but we don't have to follow them.
We are aware of the inability of ceremonies
to make us or keep us Christian.
We need Jesus Christ and His righteousness.
It is He whom we follow; He is the One whom we serve.
So much of what goes on in the name of religion
is plain garbage and should be treated as such.
We can afford to respect another man's opinions—
we are hardly capable of denying his experiences—
but if he adds to or subtracts from what God
through Christ has done for us,
then his gospel is not for us
and we ought to avoid it like the plague.

Jesus Christ is sufficient—
and so is the righteousness that He imparts to us.
We don't earn or merit or gain it by following
certain rules or rituals;
we receive it as the gift of God's love.
We possess this righteousness
even now by faith in Christ.
We have no need for any other.

This by no means indicates that we have arrived—
that we have already reached the ultimate
in our natural state of being.
We do, indeed, belong to God; we are His possession.
And yet we struggle constantly
to surrender our total beings to Him
—to let Him have His way with us.
This does not come easily.
It involves the crucible of conflict—
even failure and defeat
But even when we fall, we fall only to rise again.
Acknowledging but never nursing our failures,
we claim God's gracious forgiveness and carry on,
knowing that our loving God understands
and perpetually reaches out to draw us to Himself.
Even while we are God's sons and daughters,
we are in the process of *becoming.*
Our creation is not yet completed
and won't be until we break through this mortal shell
to become perfectly and eternally united to God.
Meanwhile our citizenship is in God's kingdom,
and we are here to advance that kingdom
throughout our sorry world.

Philippians 4

It is my fondest wish that God's children be happy.
I don't mean ecstatic or continually exuberant;
    I mean happy, full of joy,
    that deep-down contentment that persists
    even in the midst of trials and tribulations
    and difficult circumstances.
As the very children of God,
    we really don't have a thing to worry about.
Whatever our real needs,
    we know that God will fulfill them in His own time
    and in accordance with His will.
We can well afford to celebrate,
    to live in thankfulness,
    and to allow the incomprensible peace of God
    to mend the frayed edges of our troubled lives
    and make us serene and secure in our Christian faith.

It is not easy, but worthy of every effort
    to cast out the troublesome demons that plague us
    and to think and to act positively.
The unfortunate happenings that beset us
    should not cheat us out of the joy
    that comes through Christ.
We don't have to allow these things
    to come between us and our God.

Whether we are rich or poor,
    in the valley or on the mount,
    whether there be sorrow or pain
    or conflict or defeat,
    this need not threaten our relationship with God.

We belong to Him,
and if we think and act as if we belong to Him,
nothing will alter that glorious relationship.
We are His forever, and we can celebrate forever
our adoption and our identity
as His sons and daughters.
And He will provide us
with the strength and the courage
that we need to confront and overcome
anything that comes our way.

Colossians 3

I wonder if we really understand it,
    that we are the people of God,
    that He loves us and chooses that we be His people.
Now we are really alive!
As Christ was raised from the dead,
    so we have been brought from death to life,
    and we shall live forever.
We must set our hearts and fix our minds
    on this fantastic truth.
Faith means that we begin to live and act as if
    this is the truth, that this really happened,
    whether we feel it or not.

There are, however, still some things within us
    which must not be permitted
    to control our thinking or activities.
They are those things that come between us and God
    and are capable of causing harm to our fellowman.
Still rising out of the darkness to haunt and tempt us
    are the shadows of greed and lust
    and hostility and deceit,
    booby traps that can destroy us
    and anyone close to us.
We must, by God's grace and His power at work within us,
    blast these insidious demons out of our lives.
And we must do so again and again,
    for they die hard, these agents of death.

Thus we must grow in the faith,
    allowing the Spirit of God
    to captivate and subordinate

every aspect of our being under His purging love.
We must plug up these loopholes in our lives
by focusing continually upon God and His love
and permit Him to flood our hearts with His love.
And we must determinedly and actively exercise that
inflowing and outgoing love by reaching out
to others in concern and compassion.

We are to begin doing this
with those who are near us.
We must start right where we are—
even with our comrades in Christ—
by being open, honest, truthful, nonjudgmental,
manifesting patience and understanding,
forgiving them as God indeed forgives us,
allowing God's love to spill over our lives
into the troubled lives of others.
But God forbid that our love be limited
to our own kind.
It is God's love that reaches out to others
through our love,
and God's love is destined for all mankind,
the whole human family, slave and free,
rich and poor, black and white.
What we do in our interpersonal relationships
we are to do
as the children of God,
the disciples of Jesus Christ,
in the spirit of celebration and thanksgiving.

1 Thessalonians 5

Over against those generous attempts of self-appointed
prophets to predict the visible return of our Lord
are our Lord's own words informing us that His return
or reappearance will be sudden and unexpected.
And yet the final coming of Christ should be
no surprise to His faithful disciples.
We ought to be ready to meet our Lord
whatever the appointed day or hour.
It really makes little difference whether we be alive
or have already passed on to life everlasting;
when He comes we shall see Him and with Him
consummate His purposes in our world.

While we live upon this planet,
we should live as if He were already here.
Indeed, He is here! He has come!
His disappearance after His resurrection was
followed by Pentecost
And Pentecost marked, in a wonderful event,
His return to invisibly infill
and indwell the hearts of His disciples.
The way in which we can always be ready for the final
and ultimate reappearance of Christ
is not to gather on some hill in pious meditation.
It is to recognize and rely
upon the Spirit of God within us
and to extend His kingdom
through serving humanity about us.

We are to walk in faith, to serve in joy,
and to praise God whatever the circumstances
that surround us.
God grant that we may be totally His.
Then we are ever ready for His visible reappearance.

James 1

We have much to learn as the children of God.
The most difficult, perhaps, is to learn
how to regard our trials and tribulations—
even the tragedies that beset us—
as capable of enhancing and enriching our lives.
Whereas God does not send them, He does permit them,
and He can use them to draw us closer to Him
and thereby accomplish His purposes
in and through us.
We desperately need the wisdom to accept these
painful happenings with graciousness, even with joy,
knowing that whatever they may be,
God can transform them from ugliness into beauty,
from the plots of Satan designed to destroy
into the purposes of God
destined to do us good.
The key is a genuine faith in a loving God,
a faith that frees us and strengthens us
to endure whatever may come our way.

These tribulations do not come from God.
The conflicts we engage in have their origin in the
forces of evil that permeate our hemisphere
as well as in our own self-centered natures,
the rebel will that recoils from the vision of light
and freedom and sacrificial love.
We won't win every battle in this incessant war
against the powers of the night,
but the ultimate victory is,
in Jesus Christ, already ours.
If we fall only to rise again, fail only to fight again,

we discover a forgiving and loving God
indwelling our hearts and strengthening our arms
to carry on this war of the ages.
It is not difficult to see or imagine God's presence
in sunlight and success,
but it is when we recognize that God is with us
in the crucible of conflict
that we experience real joy.

Let us be aware, however,
that we can be trapped by tribulation.
If we attempt to fight our selfish, sin-ridden desires
by ourselves, we are in for defeat
and eventual destruction.
Courting those inner fires
usually resolves in getting burned.
Faith in God and in His truth and grace
will give us the edge, and the final victory,
even over our enflamed passions and foolish errors.

There is something else we must learn as God's children.
It is not enough to be listeners and proclaimers
of the Gospel;
we are commissioned to be doers.
Christian faith that falls short of loving performance
in respect to the needs of suffering people about us
falls far short of genuine faith.
May our small faith be rekindled and burn bright
with joy and obedience.

James 2

It may seem like a small matter,
but it translates as a gigantic flaw in the lives
of scores of Christians.
They dare to call themselves believers in
and followers of Jesus Christ,
and yet they act like outright bigots in their
relationships to people who cross their path.
If we look carefully—and honestly—
we may recognize this to be one of our problems,
that we are among those who talk limitlessly about
loving humanity but who are really very selective
about whom we accept as the objects
of our love and concern.
It may be expected that we be very particular about
whom we live with and confide in,
but when we show greater respect for those who are
of our race or economic status
than we do for those who are not,
we are making distinctions
that our Lord will not make.

We are enjoined to love our neighbor as ourselves.
When our judgment of people or our actions toward them
are determined by the color of their skin,
the cut of their clothes,
or the size of their bank account,
we are not acting like the children
and servants of God
—and we ought to be ashamed of ourselves.
Indeed, we are sinning against God
and endangering our relationship to Him

when we neglect to give equal respect and value
to all of His children around us.
We need to reexamine our concepts of morality,
to blast out some of the silly notions that determine
our responses to life and people,
and learn how to be loving and compassionate.

Some of us are still hooked on that ridiculous notion
that religious faith is something to be exercised
mainly through the rituals of a worship service.
We may not admit it,
but the facts speak for themselves.
We are all mouth—in terms of testimonials—
but the rest of our bodies are often paralyzed
by unbelief or disobedience.
Whatever the reason—fear or apathy or selfishness—
or the possibility that we haven't yet really
embraced God's love,
what we are demonstrating
is a far cry from Christian faith.
We need to call a spade a spade,
to tear away the window dressing,
the fictitious labels,
and have the courage to confront the painful truth
that we can't talk faith unless we have faith.
And when we have the faith
that Jesus proclaimed and demonstrated,
we, in turn, will live it and demonstrate it
in sacrificial love for the human family about us.

Let us stop playing games with God,
accepting only what suits our selfish concepts,
and embrace Him as His Word declares Him to be.
Let us serve Him by serving our fellowman.

1 Peter 1

Another way to test whether or not our faith is genuine
is to see whether we can be thankful in the midst of
trying circumstances.
Some of us suffer much in the course of our lives.
All of us are continually exposed to temptations
and tribulations that are more than we can endure.
What we must understand is that God is able to use
even these things,
the apparently unfortunate happenings that hound us,
to accomplish His purposes in and through us.
We need only consult our memory banks to confirm
how even the tragedies that shafted us in the past
have made significant contributions to our lives
and made us more lovingly sensitive to
the sorrows and pains that befall others.
The key to strength and courage, the ability to endure,
and the grace to find beauty and joy even within
the crucible experiences of our lives is faith.
And faith is demonstrated and expressed when we
dare to be thankful, to shout God's praises,
even in the middle of our problems and pressures.

It is probable that we will be forcefully separated
from many people and things that are precious to us,
and this separation will involve sorrow and pain.
The blessings and gifts
that are eternally valid, however,
will never be taken from us.
The gift of God's Son,
the eternal hope renewed in His resurrection,
the presence of His Spirit,

the salvation which is already ours—
these gifts are ours forever and ought to fill
our lives with perpetual praise.

It is important, then,
whatever happens to us in our world,
that our hope be focused firmly upon God,
and that our lives
be involved in His eternal objectives.
He is truly our Father and we are at all times
to be His obedient children and servants.
He paid the price of our redemption and adoption.
We belong to Him; we are His possessions.
May our faith,
tested constantly by the hot fires of adversity,
be enlarged and increased
May our love be made more honest and generous.
And may it be our do-or-die determination to please
God and serve our fellowman
regardless of the cost or consequence to our lives.

1 Peter 4

We ought not to be surprised when we are afflicted
by tragic or troublesome events.
What is happening in our world today—
with us and our loved ones about us—
has been the lot of all God's creatures
throughout the ages.
Jesus Christ Himself, God's beloved Son, suffered much
in the course of His brief life
upon this strife-ridden world.
How dare we expect any less?
It is, therefore, not so tragic or unfortunate
that we suffer.
It is probable that such suffering
will enrich our lives and enlarge our faith.
But God forbid that we be the cause of another's pain.
May God forgive us should this happen, and help us
to rectify our foolishness and carelessness
and subdue or lessen the suffering we have caused.

It is not possible to comprehend the fateful things
that happen from time to time.
It is not expected that we do,
only that we trust Him
who suffered on our behalf
and who will be with us in our trials and conflicts.

Sufferings, trials, conflicts come to all of us
at one time or another.
They cannot be avoided or ignored.
They are real—and they hurt.

But in addition to trusting God
in the midst of conflicts,
we can cushion their shock or lessen their hurt
by holding on to one another, by loving, sharing,
helping to bear one another's burdens and sufferings.
This is what it means to belong to the family of God.
This is one of our purposes in representing
and communicating Him in our walk upon this world.
Let us be alert to the needs of one another
and thereby help one another remain faithful to God.

2 Peter 1

Do we really believe
    that our great God has granted through His Spirit
    everything we need to be happy and contributive
    as His children and servants?
It's true!
But like money in some savings account
    God's precious gifts remain in the bank
    and our lives remain dwarfed and niggardly,
    largely dependent upon small talents
    and starved by large doubts.
Only by cashing in on God's glorious promises
    are we able to live effectively
    and productively
    in our kind of world.

There are other things
    we must stir into the divine recipe
    for joyous living in a joyless society.
A large measure of faith must be laced generously
    with kindness and goodness.
Added to that must be an ever-open mind,
    a searching, reaching grasp for truth.
Courage and fortitude,
    a dogged determination to keep going,
    a persistent, day-by-day surrender
    to God and His purposes,
    are necessary for Christian maturity.
Then there must be love—and added to love, more love,
    for this is the most important ingredient of all.
It is this that makes for authentic Christianity.

Without these qualities
our witness will have little effect
on the suffering, lonely, loveless, oppressed,
and indifferent inhabitants of this planet.

We certainly ought to be aware of these things
that are needed to make our Christian experience
genuine and permanent.
Nevertheless,
we need occasional reminders and challenges,
for, it seems, we are quick to slack off
when life becomes comfortable or the road ahead
appears a little easier to negotiate.
This may well be one of the reasons our loving God
permits suffering to afflict us;
it keeps our heads straight and our hearts focused
on the truly important goal of our lives,
a right relationship with God.

2 Peter 3

It is not surprising that we long so intensely
for the final appearance of our Lord,
for that great day when we shall be delivered
from our dissipating bodies
and destruction-bent world
to be united totally and eternally with Jesus Christ.
We live in and are threatened by a world of men
who serve themselves and who are guided
by their own self-centered passions.
They apparently have no use for God.
They act toward one another as if they were controlled
by some dark and evil force.
They kill and destroy and leave in their wake
the mangled minds and bodies
of their hapless victims.
And yet our Lord tarries;
His purposes upon this world and through us
in this world are not yet consummated.

We fearfully acknowledge the terrible things
that are happening around us
and cry out in desperation for our blessed Lord's
intervention in mankind's dark and devilish doings.
Still our Lord tarries,
and we even begin to doubt
that He will ever come again.

We need not fear or doubt.
He will come—and in His own good time.
It may be tomorrow, maybe a thousand years from now,
but He will come.

When He does come, it will be suddenly and unexpectedly
and, for the masses of men
who live by their own wills and wits,
it will be a time of final, fearful judgment.

Maybe we should regard our Lord's tarrying,
His slowness to act, in terms of purging
the wickedness of our world,
as evidence of His loving patience.
He is still waiting for men, and this may include many
of our friends and relatives,
to separate themselves
from the degradation of this planet
and return to His orbit for their lives.
The desire of His loving heart is that they, too,
will be ready to meet Him when He returns.

We do not know the year or the day or the hour.
We only know that we belong to Him.
As long as we continue
to live committed and dedicated lives
and faithfully and joyfully labor
within His purposes,
we are ready for His coming and may,
in thereby obediently serving Him and our fellowman,
bring closer that great day of His final
and ultimate revelation.

1 John 1

How do we know that life in Christ is the real thing?
Is it something we've been brainwashed to accept?
Where does God fit in?
How can we possibly swallow this irrational God-stuff
in a world of computers and satellites,
and suffering, starving, dying people?
I speak for myself, yet I can say the same
for many of you,
we know that Christ is real,
that God is alive and well and lovingly concerned
about each of us,
because we have seen Him through the eyes of faith,
have witnessed His miracles in our lives
or the lives of others around us,
and have experienced His forgiving and life-giving
love in our own hearts.
We know Him; He is real to us,
and He is the source of our joy!

It is this grand experience that we are dedicated
to share with others,
the experience of loving fellowship with God,
of reconciliation and restoration to His plan
and destiny for His children.
It is, as well, an ever-growing and enriching experience
that confirms our personal worth as God's redeemed
children and draws us into a warm and loving
relationship with one another.
Above all, it reveals to us the meaning of forgiveness,
of God's acceptance of us just as we are.

We no longer fear God's judgment,
His anger or displeasure over our sins and failures.
Our Savior, Jesus Christ, has borne that on our behalf.
Our greatest concern is that He who through Christ
accepts us as we are will ever have His way with us
and make us into everything He wants us to be.

1 John 2

Our sins and failures do not need to come
between us and God.
There will be failings from time to time;
we must recognize and acknowledge them and claim anew
the forgiveness that comes through Jesus Christ.
Then we must commit ourselves once more,
and every day of our lives,
to trust and obedience.
We can always be sure of God's acceptance;
He will never let us down.

If our commitment is genuine, however,
it will be to our Lord's pattern and style of living.
Our Lord lived by one basic commandment,
one system of morality;
it was the commandment and morality of love.
He who revealed to us His Father's love
commanded us to love, to live and serve in love.
The follower of Jesus Christ will not consciously
entertain any thoughts of bigotry or prejudice.
If he does, he will not long be a follower of Christ.
Hatred, apathy, insensitivity, bigotry, indifference,
when such characterizes attitudes and relationships
to one's fellowmen,
are the demons of darkness.
And if they are allowed to enter our lives,
they will most surely cut us off from God or betray our
professed relationship to Him to be a gigantic lie.

We must not allow our energies and affections to be
sapped by the ephemeral attractions of this world.

If this happens, it will drain us of spiritual power—
that divine energy destined for divine purposes
and expressed in loving relationships
with our fellowmen.
Jesus Christ is our Savior and Master.
He has poured out His Spirit upon us.
We must not allow anyone, whatever his intentions,
to confuse us by casting doubt
upon this splendid truth.
We are God's children,
the brothers and sisters of Jesus Christ.
If we follow Him and live as He would have us to live,
nothing can disrupt or destroy that status.

1 John 3

The fact is we are God's children now!
This status and relationship is not something
    we work for or wait for, it is ours here and now.
It is the gift and consequence of God's love.
Because of this fabulous truth,
    we need never question our identity
    or doubt our validity.
We are and shall be members of the family of God forever.

As God's children, then, we can no longer entertain
    those things that are grievous to Him.
Nor can we expend our energies or dedicate our lives
    upon those matters or projects that do not serve Him.
This does not mean that we avoid our world
    or flee from its hazards and risks.
Armored in God's grace
    and supported by the love and concern
    of our comrades,
    we, as God's soldiers and servants,
    enter into our arena of daily conflict
    to bring God's grace and love to bear
    upon the victims
    of this world's atrocities and obscenities.

Because we are God's children and servants,
    citizens of another Kingdom,
    loyal to that divine Kingdom,
    it is not surprising
    that the world regards us as aliens
    and resents our presence and ministry.

We have discovered our identity and significance
as God's children.
We do not have to be fearful
of this world's condemnations
or be dependent upon its acceptance.
Our response to its enmity is self-sacrificing love.
It may mean our eventual crucifixion as it did for
our Lord and so many of His followers.
It also means we are thereby adopting God's design
and following His destiny for our lives,
and exciting, risk-filled style of living
that guarantees freedom and joy
in the midst of this world's oppression and pain.
Above all, it means that we cease spewing platitudes
and begin to demonstrate our love for our fellowman.
When we are wide open to God and His grace
and to our fellowman and his needs,
then we know we are seeking, embracing,
and living the truth in our lives.

It is obviously not enough to make confessions
and proclamations concerning our Christian faith.
While we are saved by faith—not work—
a genuine faith in God
is clearly marked by obedience.
We live in obedience to God when,
while believing in Him,
we lovingly and actively reach out to meet the
needs of our fellowman.
Apart from this level of obedience,
one's faith is very much in question
and so one's relationship to God.

1 John 4

After all is said and done,
the proof of our adoption of God's children is love.
This begins with our acceptance of God's love
as it is revealed and granted to us
through Jesus Christ.
It is further revealed and extended through
our love for one another.
This is what the God-life is all about.
Apart from God there is no real love;
apart from love God is not real in us
and is not able to work through us.
If we assume we can continue to bask in God's love
even while we harbor hateful or unloving thoughts
about a brother or sister,
we are deceiving ourselves.

We live in a fear-ridden world and we foolishly allow
these fears to permeate our lives and polarize us
in our interpersonal relationships.
If God's love truly dominates our lives
this will not happen because it crowds out all fear
and unites us to God and to each other.
God's love is perfect—and He loves perfectly.
This is the manner in which He loves us.
Not only should this free us from the fears
that plague our world, but free us to love
our fellowman without concern for consequences.
This is our assignment in our world today,
to be, as was Christ in His visible visitation,
love incarnate in a love-starved society.
Let us begin by genuinely loving one another.